SELF TALK

FOR PEAK PERFORMANCE AND RESULTS

Terri Andres

HARVESTER PUBLISHING
ATLANTA, GA

Copyright © 2023 by Terri Andres.

All rights reserved. No part of this publication may be reproduced, distributed or transmitted in any form or by any means, including photocopying, recording, or other electronic or mechanical methods, without the prior written permission of the publisher, except in the case of brief quotations embodied in critical reviews and certain other noncommercial uses permitted by copyright law. For permission requests, write to the publisher, addressed "Attention: Permissions Coordinator," at the address below.

Terri Andres/Harvester Publishing
4780 Ashford Dunwoody Rd
Atlanta, GA 30338
harvester-publishing.com

Book cover design by Tanya Prokop

Ordering Information:
Special discounts are available on bulk quantity purchases by small groups, organizations, associations and others. For details, contact the publisher at the above website.

Self Talk / Terri Andres. —1st ed.
ISBN 978-1-7351862-1-4

Contents

Introduction 9
Part 1: Fresh Insight About Words 11
Part 2: Transforming Your Self Talk 21
Part 3: The 5-Week Challenge 39
Day 1: The Best Part of Me 47
Day 2: The Place Where I Belong 49
Day 3: Peace is My Inheritance 51
Day 4: Staying in My Lane 53
Day 5: Soul Currency 55
Day 6: Beyond Choosing Joy 57
Day 7: The Word as Bread 59
Day 8: Habitual Mental Checkup's 61
Day 9: Forget the Status Quo 63
Day 10: Modus Operandi X 65
Day 11: In the New 67
Day 12: Being Spiritually Minded 69
Day 13: The Way Up is Down 71
Day 14: Where Freedom Is 73
Day 15: Matters of the Heart 75
Day 16: Receiving Glory 77

Day 17: Increasing Glory 79
Day 18: Crowned with Glory 81
Day 19: Called to Glory 83
Day 20: The Image of Glory 85
Day 21: Flesh and Bones 87
Day 22: My Superior Self 89
Day 23: The Spirit of Life 91
Day 24: Receiving Holy Spirit 93
Day 25: Experiencing Holy Spirit 95
Day 26: Bodily Sacrifice 97
Day 27: Produce and Performance 99
Day 28: A Necessary Exchange 101
Day 29: Training My Body 103
Day 30: Conditioning My Soul 105
Day 31: Singing Words in My Heart 107
Day 32: Speaking Words of Truth 109
Day 33: Keeping Watch Over My Words 111
Day 34: Activating My Spirit 113
Day 35: Praying Without Ceasing 115
Part 4: Conclusion 117
   The Way Forward 118

About The Author 123

Dedicated to my husband, Hal, whom I love and adore and who challenges me to be my highest and best self in every way, including self talk.

My words are spirit and life

—JESUS CHRIST

Introduction

Right off the bat I want you to know this book has a spiritual center and spiritual agenda. The goal of this book is to make you more spiritual by the words you speak. Let me repeat that word by word so it sinks in better. The goal of this book is: To. Make. You. More. Spiritual. By. The. Words. You. Speak. To make your entire self – what I refer to as 3B Self™ being, body, behavior – more spiritual. By the words you speak.

At this point you are probably asking questions such as why should I become more spiritual? Why is this important? Why does it matter? What major difference will this make for myself and my life and my circumstances? I am glad you asked.

The more spiritual you become, the more powerful you become and the more self-control you possess. Power begets self-control. Read that again.

When we lack self-control, we lack or are weak in personal power and thus react and respond poorly in the heat of a moment when we need to exercise self-control versus lose control and find ourselves in a regretful state of being or regretful situations and circumstances.

Spiritual beings are able to exist and act from a position of power and self-control.

Power and self-control over evil thoughts. Over negative words. Over ill feelings. Over ill cravings. Over responding in kind when someone upsets you. Over intentional or accidental offenses (aka forgiveness). Over thinking and acting irrationally when unwanted situations and circumstances arise. And on and on and on.

The promised "peak performance and results" from the subtitle will first and foremost make you more spiritual in your 3B

Self™. Once you become more spiritual, the conventional high achiever performance and results from exercising self-discipline, developing familiar success habits and by grinding through long and hard workdays, will naturally manifest. So it's a win-win. Becoming more spiritual, which is what your being, body and behavior *needs* and becoming a high performer that produces results, which is what your being, body and behavior *wants*.

Finally, as a little fun fact, I chose an image of a blue butterfly for the book cover because butterflies represent transformation and blue is the color of grace. I want you to know, believe and receive the fact that there is a space of grace carved out especially for your transformation into your highest and best self. All that is needed from you to start this journey is desire. Then discipline. The way you use words being one of those disciplines. Which is major.

Terri Andres

Part 1: Fresh Insight About Words

Let's dive right in and talk about what words are. First and foremost, words are spiritual which make them superior to the physical realm – the primary realm we exist and operate in. Everything you see and everything you know in this physical realm is because of words. And it is because of this that words themselves are life. *Words are life.* This is a big truth. Meditate on it until it begins to resonate with your spirit. Wait for it. It eventually will.

The Spiritual Nature of Your Words

Words are spiritual because they come from God. God is a Spirit. Words are also spiritual because they are unseen. They are abstract, immaterial and intangible. They exist and act in the unseen, spiritual realm.

Just like words cannot be seen, they cannot be touched. They exist and operate outside the realm of our physical senses and exist and operate solely in the spiritual, unseen realm which – catch this – is superior to the seen realm. Keyword *superior*. The unseen realm is superior to the seen realm because everything seen first exists in the unseen realm as a thought then is communicated through words that give life to thoughts that, in turn, become living things. Remember our big truth from the previous page that words themselves are life? This section just unpacked this big truth.

Becoming More Spiritual by The Words You Speak

I shared in the introduction the main goal of this book is to make you more spiritual by the words you speak. With this, it is fitting to address the *why* question I am sure is at the forefront of your mind at this point. *Why is becoming more spiritual important?* Here's why:

The more spiritual you are, the more like God you are. God is a Spirit.

Read that last short paragraph aloud multiple times until you start to feel the truth of it resonate within you.

The more spiritual you are, the more like God you are because God is a Spirit and you are a spirit existing in a physical body.

The more spiritual you are, the more whole you are. The more spiritual you are, the more empowered you are. The more spiritual you are, the freer you are. The more spiritual you are, the more your being, body and behavior, or 3B Self™, aligns with your highest and best self – the vision of the person you see yourself as doing all the things you see yourself doing.

Realize this. The innumerable noble pursuits of man past, present and future are ultimately to make us more like God. Let this sink in. In every pursuit, wholeness is what we are really after and, again, the more spiritual we are the more whole we are.

Now let's make it personal. The more spiritual *you* become, the more whole you become. Unseen bondages begin to loosen. Unseen chains begin to break. You experience breakthroughs and freedom and become empowered to move forward.

You are able to soar and, by default, you begin to operate at your peak level of performance which will produce massive results in your being first and, in turn, your life.

Are you at this point feeling compelled at the notion of becoming more spiritual like God, who is your Maker? If not, I encourage you to ponder over this more. Ponder becoming more spiritual – becoming whole inside, experiencing breakthrough, being free and empowered in every aspect of your being and actions – just by the words you speak. Before moving on, put the book down and allow these thoughts to resonate and speak to the depths of your soul.

Understanding Key Distinctions Between Your Words

It is important to know there are primarily two categories of words. Words that *create* and words that *communicate*. The words you use will create something or communicate something.

Words that create are meant to manifest something that does not already exist or does not exist in relation to your being and/or your life. This could be something abstract in nature like manifesting belief or courage within yourself or something material in nature like a product or piece of furniture. Two very minor examples of an infinite number of major and minor things that could be cited.

The other category, words that communicate, are meant to exchange information and knowledge. This communication exchange runs the gamut of significant to insignificant. An example of a significant communication would be someone verbalizing step by step instructions in a life-or-death situation. An example of insignificant communication would be someone shooting the breeze, being silly, cracking jokes while talking to a friend.

Realizing the distinction between the words we use is important stuff. It matters. Anything that affect outcomes matter greatly. So don't just read this and forget about it. Take it to heart. Internalize it so it can remain impressed upon your heart from henceforth, and so it stays in your subconscious and as a result you will begin to automatically recall the type of communication your choice of words are at any given time, and in doing so have some degree of control over your current reality while framing future realities.

My hope from this is you will form a habit of asking yourself questions like, are my words creative right now? If so, I better make sure I am speaking that which I want to call forth. Are my words right now words more communicative and therefore don't have strong ramifications if I am loose with them?

Asking these questions and acting accordingly from your answers to them are absolute game-changers during moments when it matters most. Like when dealing with your spouse, parenting your children, responding to your boss, resolving conflict with a friend, and of course your own self talk amid crisis. Just to name a few.

Knowledge is power and now that you are equipped with this knowledge you will be empowered to choose your words wisely.

When provoked, you will be strong enough to choose the right words instead of the wrong words that are usually the first to come to our fallen minds.

How "Your Words Are Powerful"

I put this in quotes because we have all heard it hundreds of times. And its is absolutely true. Words do carry power. We know this. But have you ever wondered about *the how* in the power of words? I have.

How are words powerful? What is it that gives them their power? The power to create and destroy. The power of life and death and everything in between.

From a biblical worldview, which millions subscribe to, words get their power from the Source of all creation and life – Yahweh. In the beginning, God *said*, as in spoke words. God, who is a Spirit, spoke and by the power (keyword) of His words the universe leapt into existence. Further, the bible teaches there is no separating Yahweh from His word. God *is* His word and since He is All-Powerful, His words are full of power.

From a humanistic worldview, words have power because of the meaning they carry. Words carry power because of the meaning they carry. Words carry meaning that affect us – our internal selves and external experience in the world—in profound ways. This is one of the reasons why if someone calls you or a loved one a bad name, you are immediately offended and fly off the handle.

Through these two polarized lenses, we see both spiritual and natural realities to words and their power. This is very important to know and keep top of mind about words, their spiritual and natural characteristics.

Of course, our objectives center around the spiritual. As they should. Because [ponder this question]:

How long will we continue to neglect spiritual matters related to ourselves?

It is high time we course correct. Here, we are on the right track. Let's take this journey together. Convicted and committed to grow spiritually, starting with our choice of words.

The Vitality of Words in General

I know I keep going here but stay with me. I am intentionally being a bit repetitive while also going a bit deeper. So lean in closer.

Words are life. Words are life and they produce life. Without words – written and spoken – life as we know it would cease. Ruminate over this and you will see its truth.

Because words themselves are life, they vital to sustaining life as we know and experience it in **THESE BODIES™**. They form languages that enable us to communicate and relate to each other.

If there was no such thing as words, there would be no comprehension, no education, no innovation and no progress in anything because there would be no effective enough means to communicate our thoughts and ideas and, in turn, materialize them.

Without words, we would be dumbfounded. We would be speechless. We would be stuck. We would be separate. And we would die quick, premature deaths.

Spoken and written words create, promote and sustain life and aside from their vitality for life and our basic human experience, they have tremendous creative power.

Energetic, locomotive power that move us. Motivate us. Strengthen us. Weaken us. Build us. Destroy us. Heal us. Hurt us and the list goes on.

Defining Power in The Context of Words

Because *power* means a lot of things, my definition of power in the context of words is *the belief, thoughts and intention of your words and your use of them*. Both written words and spoken but mostly spoken because this is a book about self talk.

Really catch this. Your beliefs and intentions determine the energy, authority and rule — or *power* — of significant words you speak. Let me repeat that. Your beliefs and intentions determine the energy, authority and rule — which make up the power — of significant words you speak. Significant words that carry creative intentions as opposed to idle words that act as couriers for basic communication exchanges.

Therefore, we have these dynamics at work when we use words: belief, intention, energy, authority and rule. And they create specific outcomes inherent to themselves.

For example, the following statements: *Jesus Christ is the Son of God and my personal Lord and Savior; I do not feel like going to work today; My nose is too big and ugly; I am scared of cockroaches; I hate exercising; I love cooking and eating food; I have fear of flying in an airplane; You make me sick and get on my nerves; I hate you; I love you; You are a mean and selfish person; She is obnoxious; He is weird and stupid; etc.*

All these statements are said from certain beliefs and carry either good or evil intentions that determine the energy of the words, that determine the rule and authority of the words, which create specific outcomes. This is *how* words are so powerful.

The Key Truths About Words (Summarized)

Realizing the mental resistance that will naturally form in your thoughts from all this "spiritual stuff", I think it will be tremendously helpful for me to summarize the key spiritual truths that have been brought forth thus far about words.

Too, acknowledging lists are always good for quick reference and repetitious reading enhances comprehension, I also decided to include this summary because, while we only covered a few facts about words, they are *big truths you need to grasp*. Go further and study out these truths by reading the noted scripture references:

- Words themselves are life (*see John 6:63*)
- Words are life-giving (*see Matthew 4:4, John 6:63*)

- Words provide vital nourishment to our spiritual beings like food provides vital nourishment to our natural, physical bodies (see John 6:35-58)
- Words carry meaning that affect **Our 3B Self™**, being/body/behavior (see Luke 6:45)
- Words are creative, forceful and powerful in that they build and destroy (see Proverbs 18:21)
- Words in and of themselves are spiritual in nature, although they very much have a natural, scientific aspect to them such as sound (see John 6:63)
- Words are living creative abstract organisms that produce and manifest material substance (see John 1:14)

The significance of words is wrapped up in their creative power. When we speak, we are creating. Creating something good (life) or creating something bad (death). Producing or destroying. Death and life are indeed in the power of our tongues.

Why Speak at All?

A lot of ground has been covered in this short section, and out of everything covered, I have saved what I consider to be the two brightest and best big truths about words for last.

The second to last big truth about words I want to leave you with answers the question of why we need to speak the Word of God versus just having the Word in our heart? This is profound so lean in close and stay with me through the repetition (it is intentional).

When we speak, we are like God. When we speak His words, His truth, we are agreeing (keyword) with Him. Agreeing with His truth. Agreeing with truth. Agreeing with His nature. His character.

Alignment with His nature. Alignment with His character. Unification. Joining with. At one with Him.

We are speaking Life. We are speaking Wisdom. We are speaking Good. We are speaking the very words and Being of God because there is no separation between God and His words.

When we speak God/His words, sound and utterance manifests His words (read that again until it sinks in). The Words of God are creative. They perform that which they are intended to do.

In the same way, since we are made in His image and likeness, we speak what is in our heart and when we speak what is in our heart, we ultimately create what we are speaking.

So if we are speaking the Word that is in our heart, we are creating a reality that aligns us with God. His Person. His image. His nature. His truth. His character. His virtue. His power. His works. His everything.

The words we speak align us and bind us to the creativity of the words.

So if we consistently speak the Word of God, we are aligning and binding ourselves to whatever the words we are speaking will render.

The creative cadence of spoken words is:
1. Speak
2. Agree
3. Align
4. Bind
5. Create

The words we speak are evidence of our agreement with what we are speaking and this aligns our being to what we are speaking.

When the words are spoken, these utterances bind our being to the creative outcomes of the words.

The Testimony of Words

Drum roll please. And now for the final big truth about words I will share in this first part of the book. For God's Word (Logos written words and Rhema words He speaks through His Spirit) and our spoken words (the significant words we speak as opposed to idle, empty vain words), consider the points that follow as the big pretty bow that ties everything together. Why it all matters. Here it is:

- The Word of God is His testimony.
- This testimony is that of Truth versus the deception mostly everything in this world is based on.
- Our responsibility is to receive God's Testimony/Truth into our hearts through our belief of it.
- When the Testimony/Truth of God is in our hearts, we stand on it. We speak it. And we act on it.
- Believing, speaking and acting on the Testimony/Truth of God transforms us from natural men to spiritual men.
- Because God's Testimony/Truth/Word is Spirit and Life.
- When we are spiritual men, we are most like Him/His image.
- We become glorious beings like Him for He is Glorious.
- Being glorious spiritual beings like Him, we worship Him in Spirit and in Truth.
- By constantly putting to death our old self/nature/man – the misdeeds of our bodies of sin.

All through the avenue of words. God's Word and words we speak. Just wow. This is deep revelation friends. **PLEASE GET THIS.**

Part 2: Transforming Your Self Talk

By now, hopefully, you have finished reading part one of this book which shares vital spiritual knowledge and revelation about words. If you skipped ahead and are starting here, I strongly recommend you go back and read part one as this is the knowledge framework in which the main objective of self talk – to make you more spiritual by the words you speak – is set in.

This knowledge awakens you to the spiritual aspect of words which, in turn, affects your use of them which, in turn, profoundly affects your internal being and everything else external to your being – situations, circumstances, experiences and outcomes.

All of this to say, again, go back and read part one if you have not done so already. It is short so spend a little more time on any section you don't catch on the first pitch (i.e., from your initial reading of it). Reread it and ponder over it. Then come back here.

This part of the book is all about *you*. Your words and words in relation to you.

Primarily, how you currently use words and transforming your self-talk using words as the major avenue. Secondly, manifestation. Manifestation of specific spiritual outcomes, chiefly becoming more spiritual. Sound good? Let's get to it.

The Privilege of Words

This is a great place to start. One thing I have come to realize while writing this book (for over two years now) is we need to increase our awareness of words in general. When I say we I am referring to humanity. We need to recognize and truly be awed by the following truth:

Man has been given the privilege to speak.

If you didn't know, now you know! Let me tell you, when I got this download from heaven, it was a complete mic drop. Bomb revelation I had never realized until that moment.

Process this for a minute before moving on. That you have been given the privilege to speak by using words. No other living creature speaks by using words. Think about this!

So why is it that humans/humanity/Man has been given this awesome privilege? Because we are made in the image and likeness of our Maker and Creator, God, and He uses words. In fact, He spoke and the earth leapt into existence. And here we are today.

Furthermore, within the privilege of speaking words, we need to be a lot more cognizant of the varying uses of words and in this cognition allow it to guide us into making the best choices when it comes to our word selection and equally important is exercising silence. Not speaking. Choosing to not use words because of their power to build and destroy.

What Exactly is Self Talk?

If I had to come up with a surface-level, standard definition, Self Talk is your personal relationship with words and how you use them when communicating with yourself and with others. But there's more to it. Much more. Here's the thing:

Our words are a reflection of our character.

Let this truth really sink in. Your words reflect your character. My character. All our character. Our maturity. Our mindset. Our virtue or lack thereof. The choice of words we use are an indication of our any and everything. And, as I've shared several times now in different sections, our words determine our actions, or behavior, toward ourselves and toward others.

Because our words are such a grandiose display of our character, we should care much and be greatly concerned about our self talk. And from this care and concern, give the rightful attention and intention to our self talk.

Can you see how our self talk creates opportunity for us to be/become better? Better in character. To grow in godliness – which means like character to God – by the way we use our words. To become like God by speaking His words. And by receiving His words and obeying His words by His word, the Word of God.

Before moving on I want you to not just comprehend this truth but to also apprehend this truth, which is to lay ahold of it so you will "get it" and keep it top of mind for the rest of your natural life.

So, allow me to share some practical application of our words and our character. If you are (or maybe you know someone that is) constantly gossiping or speaking ill of people or someone in particular, this is a reflection of the gossiper's character.

If you or you know someone who is always cracking jokes about obese people, this is a reflection of character. Maybe you are constantly making sexual references in normal conversation totally unrelated to sex but you always find a way to sexualize the subject.

Maybe you or someone you know is extremely negative and antagonistic about everything. All these applications boil down to character.

Disclaimer. Know that I am not discounting deep hurts, mental head-trips and the like. We all know pain and mental health issues are real life. While character could certainly be a factor also, these situations would have a different evaluation.

What Are You Saying to Yourself?

Again, essentially, self talk is how you communicate with yourself. It is your choice of words. The words you choose to speak and equally important the words you choose not to speak because you know they will ultimately produce death in some form.

(Note if my last statement about producing death strikes you as too strong, this indicates you have not fully absorbed the truths about words from part one of the book. I encourage you to pause here and go back and reread part one until more of the truths I am dropping resonate.)

When you are ready to move on, here are some key questions for you to ask yourself and answer in a journal or notes app:

- What do I think and say to myself repeatedly?
- What do I think and say to myself about others?
- Overall, do I use my words intentionally?
- Do I care about the words I speak or am I nonchalant?
- Do I really believe the words I speak have the power of life or death in them?

In order to answer these questions as honest as possible, it is helpful to know where the words you speak come from. Now notice I did not write *where words come from*. Rather, I wrote *where the words you speak come from.* The key distinction being *the words you speak.* Let's find out in this next section.

The Root of *Your* Words

Have you ever given serious thought to where the words you speak come from? In other words, what determines your words? Again, the key distinction being your words not words in general.

There are a couple key factors that determine the words you speak. The first and biggest is what you hear. What you hear determines the words you speak. In a later section I will unpack the connection between hearing and speech.

The second factor is what you see. What you see. What you gaze upon. What you look at. This also includes what you read.

Your eyes and ears are not only gateways to your soul but they are the two major ways you learn and process information. Think about it. If you could neither hear or see, how would you be able to learn and process intangible, intellectual information that enables your mind to develop? You can't.

So understand the words you speak come from words (isn't that interesting, your words come from other words) you hear and see through your ears and eyes. Your intellect then processes these words and forms and continually fit them into your belief and value system which form your perspectives.

But something else happens when you hear and see words. Spiritually, they are seeds that seep into your soul, take root and in the right time form (manifest) fruit which is then released through your thoughts which lead to utterance (i.e., the words you speak).

Know that right now, right now in this very moment, spiritually, there are an innumerable number of seeds in your soul from your eye and ear gates that are germinating. Whether your words are good (life) or evil (death) depends on whether the fruit that your soul produces is good or evil.

Let this sink in and ask yourself this important question. Will the seeds germinating in my soul produce life or will they produce death when I speak, according to Proverbs 4:21 which teaches us death and life are in the power of the tongue?

Your Responsibility When It Comes to Your Words

I just talked about this a few sections ago but feel it warrants repeating here. Yes, because repetition is one way we learn but, what's more is the fact that we cannot talk about responsibility without talking about privilege. They are inextricably linked.

As I've already shared, Man has been given the privilege to speak words. No other creature uses words. Only man. Only humanity has been given the privilege to speak and use words. Other creatures communicate through sound and some kind of utterance but none of them use words. I need you to catch this and comprehend the significance of it. Ponder and when you have, hopefully you will be in awe at the privilege you and I have of speaking words.

With privilege comes responsibility.

Our responsibility – really catch this – is to speak words that are good. Words that build up. Words that edify. To create with our words. To not destroy with our words. To not curse with our words. To not speak idle words. Rather our words ought to be fruit-bearing unto the rendering of some kind of future harvest depending on the words sown.

Now is a good time to pause for a sort of programming note. Know that what I am imparting here is not some "name it and claim it" hocus pocus that is rooted in evil, ungodly gain for the glory of self. What I am referring to is your vocabulary and word choices in times when it really counts in a significant way.

Furthermore, what I am trying to drive home here is patterning ourselves after our Creator and Maker, Jehovah God, by forming a discipline (keyword) and practice (keyword) around our self talk. Let me repeat that louder for the people in the back:

This is patterning ourselves after our Creator and Maker by forming a discipline and practice around our self talk.

This is spiritual discipline and spiritual practice that makes us more like, or better said, akin, to God our Father who is Spirit and life (catch the spirit and life part; that true life is life in the spirit not this natural only life most of you reading this have been living) and created the heavens and the earth and everything in between past, present and future through the creative power of words.

Speaking good and godly words and thereby aligning with good and godly principles of sowing and reaping and seedtime and harvest should be an earnest desire of our hearts and thus our striving. Ponder over this. Locate your heart in this respect.

We should care about our use of words like we care about external attributes of our selves (i.e., our looks, our body, our hair, our teeth and other aspects of our physical appearance). Wouldn't that be something? If we cared about our words as much or more than we care about our physical appearances. To make our spoken words to ourselves and others as excellent as possible. To give our words a great workout, you know what I mean? #micdrop

When we speak, we are creating. Creating something good (life-giving) or creating something bad (death). Producing or destroying.

The creative aspect of words is why they are powerful. I repeat, the creative aspect of words is why they are so powerful.

The Power Struggle with Your Words

I covered this briefly in part one, but this is a subject that warrants repeating because power in the context of your words is imperative to understand.

> *In order to transform your self talk, you must be awake to the way power is at work in you.*

What kind of power you ask? The power of good or the power of evil.

Realize power in this context is a force that is always in operation. Always. As in always. Incessant. Never ceasing. And because good and evil are dichotomous, their power can never operate simultaneously. Either the power of good is working or the power of evil is working. One or the other but never both at a given time.

With this, realize the words you speak (among other things, but our topic is words) are the result of the power at work in you. You will speak good words when the power of good is at work in you or you will speak evil words when the power of evil is at work in you.

Practically and strategically, power comes after your decision. How so? In a word, action. Action is energy which is what power is. Power follows decision. Whatever you will to do you do because your very will empowers you to take action.

Your decision will be good (actions aligned with good) or evil (actions aligned with evil). This is power in play.

Know there is a very prevalent and pervasive power struggle for your very being - 3B Self™ being, body and behavior. To behave in alignment with good (godly) or behave in alignment with evil (ungodly).

Another thing about power is what it is in and of itself. Power is *power*. Power is *power*.

Power is a forceful driving force that drives something - whether that something is a person (you) or a thing like a motor. Power is a force of energy that determines a course of action. Please hear me here. Power is a force of energy that creates a course of action.

Understand that good power in operation creates a good course of action that will produce a good result. Good fruit. Likewise, evil power in operation creates an evil course of action that will produce an evil result. Rotten fruit.

The power at work in you will produce good or evil outcomes. The power at work in you will produce good or evil self talk. Period. There is no in-between. There is no grey area to this. It is black and white.

All that being said, the final thought I want to leave you with is this: you get to choose. You get to decide on the power that will operate in you. How? By your words. By the good or evil story you tell yourself at any and every given moment. The good or evil story you tell yourself about how you feel in any given moment. The good or evil story you tell yourself about that other person, be it your spouse, child, sibling, parent, boss, friend or whoever. Choose well. Choose wise.

New and Different Self-Discipline with Your Words

What will help us with our words is self-discipline. We must discipline ourselves to speak words of life.

To some degree, you (all of us) already use self-discipline in the words you speak. So this is an invitation to use self-discipline to speak words of life, the key phrase here being *words of life*. To not only speak good about ourselves and others. To not only avoid speaking evil about ourselves and others. But to actually speak words of life. Words that produce life.

The only way we can be successful at taming and training our tongues for this is if we are spiritual. If we are more spiritual than we are natural. Because whatever is dominant wins.

Equally important, we must develop a new self-discipline, which is the skill of not speaking, especially when provoked. Not speaking idle words is just as important as speaking creative words.

Developing the self-discipline to not speak is a very big challenge. The book of James in the Bible tells us how difficult it is to control our tongues. But it can be done with practice (key phrase *with practice*).

Self-talk and equally important self-silence.

Don't allow your words to weigh you down and destroy and defeat you. Or destroy and defeat others.

Discipline your self talk to use words aright. And in this current vain we've been in, one strategy for speaking the right words is simply speaking less. When you don't speak too much you lessen your chances of saying the wrong things. Stop talking so much. Be a man or a woman of few words. This is virtue.

Yet another strategy is to practice (keyword) self talk. After reading this book and receiving the revelations, be willing and intentional about starting over. To reset the relationship you have with words.

Our Words are the Result of our Spiritual Condition

Disclaimer. I am going to be a little redundant here but bear with me, it will be worth it.

Recall when I was shared shortly ago that our words reflect our character. Right? Let's go deeper.

Really know and get that your self talk is an outflow of what is within you. The most significant desires/cravings/appetites etc., whatever is in your soul.

Which is to say, our self talk is the outflow of our spirit/soul/heart. Our desires/appetite/cravings. Our thoughts that become words (utterance). Our actions that become our habits that become routine (good habits) or addictions (bad habits).

Really all these can be summarized as our spiritual condition. Your spiritual condition. Think about it. Locate yourself. What is your current spiritual condition? Take the time to do an honest evaluation of your condition in each of these areas. You will never conquer what you don't truthfully (keyword) confront.

Realize this important truth:

Our words are the result of our spiritual condition.

The condition of our soul -- what is in our heart (desires, appetite, cravings), mind, will, emotions, intellect and imagination – determines the condition of our being, body and behavior.

A natural man or woman will speak words of the world that will work (keyword) to make them more natural/carnal in being, body and behavior. A spiritual man or woman will speak words of the spirit and thus work to make them more spiritual in being, body and behavior. Remember, the more spiritual you become the more like God you are!

Using Your Words Better

Generally, when you know better you do better. Generally, when you have the right (keyword) knowledge, you operate right. You make the right choice. You make the right decision.

This helps explain why most of us are so careless and reckless with our words.

Because when we don't know the power of our words and how we use them. When we don't understand the influence of our words. When we don't understand the impact of our words. When we don't understand the creative power of our words to build or destroy, we misuse and abuse words because there is no anchor, aim, meaning or purpose to our words.

On the other hand, when we do understand all these things, we use our words wisely as Proverbs 31:26 encourages us to do.

We begin to speak less because we are more careful of what we say, understanding whatever we say will ultimately, directly or indirectly, produce life or death in some shape, form or fashion.

Doing The Work for Using Your Words Better

On the practical side, this book is a *tool* for transformation. Tools are used to get necessary jobs done. Each of the book's components were thoughtfully crafted and included to help you use your words to change your world by first and foremost changing your 3B Self™ (being/body/behavior). And second, to change your world – the life you experience outside of your self (your situations, circumstances, relationships, service, livelihood etc).

> *As you begin to speak the right words, they will begin to produce Zoé, the life of God (Spirit) within you.*

Living a *Zoé* life is living a life that is characterized by unconditional love for others. Overflowing joy. Overflowing peace. Patience. Kindness. Gentleness. Humility. Self-control. Self-discipline. Service. Creativity and productivity that ushers you into living purposefully and thereby fulfilling your maximum potential.

Further, as you become more spiritual, your power to forgive begins to increase while being easily offended decreases. How many of you know that walking in forgiveness is paramount to a life lived well and something that we *all* need more of?

Please do not take these statements lightly. What has been brought forth here is the awesome, supernatural reality and victory you can experience.

How? As you work your way through this book and apply this knowledge to yourself and life beyond. Starting with self talk.

Are you excited and eagerly anticipating wonderful outcomes in the areas you need them most? I hope your answer is an enthusiastic *yes* and it is my honor to be beside you on this journey.

Incorporating Strategy for Using Your Words Better

Now that we have covered the spiritual aspect of words in great depth, we need to cover strategies to start speaking right.

OUT OF YOUR HEART AND MIND

Here's the thing, you cannot start speaking right until you start thinking right. Let me repeat that. You cannot start speaking right until you start thinking right.

Now is a good time to recall where your thoughts come from. Your thoughts come from what is in your heart and soul, the very core of your being where your desires, appetite and convictions live. With this, the wisdom of proverbs 4:23 teaches us out of the heart flows the issues of life. And Jesus taught us out of the abundance of the heart the mouth speaks. All of this to say, whatever is in your heart is what determines your words.

To oversimplify it, the order for how your words form is this: heart, mind, words. Your thoughts (mindset) form around what is in your heart and these thoughts are expressed through the words you speak.

Said another way, what is in you determines the words you speak.

> *If you really want to discover, or uncover, what is in you, pay attention to your speak. Your conversation reveals what is in you.*

If you want to speak the right words, know right words come from right thoughts and thoughts are based on what is in our heart and what is in our heart is determined by what we continually see and what we continually hear.

This boils down to our consumption/intake through our eye and ear gates – the two major gateways to our soul (mind, will, emotions, imagination and intellect). These thoughts, then, form your belief systems which determine your words and your actions/your behavior.

With this, you must evaluate the voice or voices you hear/give attention to and assess whether the voice is one of truth or one of deception. If the voice is that of truth then you will have the right thoughts and thus speak the right words. If the voice is that of deception you will have wrong thoughts and belief systems and thus speak wrong words that will directly and indirectly work to manifest destruction for yourself and/or others.

Can I just say it? Wondering if by now you see it too. That all this revelation can be summed up with one word: Righteousness. Righteousness of heart is the ultimate strategy for self talk.

PROVERBS 31:26

Now knowing how the words you speak are produced, go back and assess your words. Further, assess them considering this bible verse that instructs us to speak wisely[1].

Start by considering your consumption, ear and eye. What have you been hearing? Whose voice are you listening to? What have you been seeing, what have you been watching? Is most of what you been seeing digital entertaining images from streaming tv, movies, TikTok, Instagram, Facebook, YouTube or the like.

Have you been seeing any text? You know, written words in books or the like. Remember these things called textbooks that used to be our primary source of consumption for learning and comprehension? Of course, I am being a bit facetious but I hope it is working and you well see my point.

Tragically, most of what we are doing is entertaining ourselves and overwhelming and damaging our senses because our brains were not designed to consume the volume of digital images we are by in large consuming. The statistics are astounding and tragic and, honestly, pathetic. We are all guilty and we all need to do better.

Putting and Keeping Yourself on the Hook

How easily we make exceptions for ourselves to be reckless in our use of words. I feel the sting of this truth as I write it because I know how guilty I am.

Especially when we are offended. Especially when our emotions are running wild. Especially when we respond based on some fear. Especially when we are trying to control another person or control a situation or circumstance. Especially when we try to control some other type of outcome.

We know what is right. We know the right road we should travel, but because of our own pride, ego, haughtiness, wants you name it. Because we have self at the center, we make exceptions and we act in error, unbecoming and outside the character of Christ. The power of evil in full effect.

Am I right? Have you been here? I have. Too much. And, again, as I type this I am starting to weep because this should not be. Let's change this. Let's all work individually and collectively to change this and be more responsible with our words. Amen.

What Our Words Ought to Be

When it really counts, we ought to be speaking spiritual words that are full of spiritual truth. When we speak and believe the words we are speaking and the words we are hearing from our speak, we begin to transform from natural to spiritual. The Bible teaches faith comes by hearing. There is a profound speaking and hearing connection. Speaking and hearing work together.

This process is completely opposite of what most of humanity naturally does, which is speak words that are nothing more than idle (versus intentional) and result in any and everything related to the spirit of this world and all its evil activity and endings.

Food for thought. Christ deems the words we speak that do not lead to eternal life as idle words. Worthless words. Merely human and natural words that do not profit anything in the context of true life which is eternal life here and hereafter.

Therefore. Therefore. Our words. Your words. Should be such that you (we) become more spiritual – and thereby more powerful – because of your (our) words.

The question, then, becomes what should our spoken words be or be like? The answer is, we ought to speak the Word of God, and sing it too for that matter. We ought to speak Christ's words, which are words that give life, edify, strengthen and heal. Our words should always be good.

However, too much, the reality is we speak evil words of death, destruction, division, hatred, selfishness and so on.

This book, the insight and the challenge, aims and is able to change this. #CallToAction

Notes

[1] I purposely did not include the words to this verse of scripture and others I've referenced to encourage you to go further than reading here and look them up on your own.

Part 3: The 5-Week Challenge

When I was inspired to write this book, my chief objective was to create a resource that would, with commitment and consistency, make you more spiritual just by the words you speak. Emphasis on *just by*, which is to say, to significantly transform yourself just by the way you use your words.

Now that, from a knowledge standpoint, you know why becoming more spiritual is important and how this happens through the avenue of words, the next necessary step in transformation is to put this knowledge into practice.

> *This challenge is where the rubber meets the road. Where knowledge meets practical application.*

As you will see in the next section about the mechanics of the challenge, it was and is designed with the specific purpose to make you more spiritual by the words you speak. It is designed for spiritual conditioning. To spiritually condition your heart, mind, and words which, in turn, will affect the totality of your being, body and behavior, or 3B Self™ as I've coined it.

Last, but most important here, is a callout around belief. I need you to believe it is possible to become more spiritual just by using your words. I need you to believe successfully completing this challenge will result in you being more spiritual. *You* (keyword) need to believe it is possible to become more spiritual just by using your words.

Which ultimately translates to – really hear what I am expressing here and catch it – being conformed more into the image of Christ (who is a Spirit) which begets wholeness and freedom from hurts, habits, hang-ups. Freedom from unforgiveness and offense. Freedom from anger and addictions. Freedom from other self-sabotaging behaviors. You will increase in personal power and self-control and self-discipline and all the fruits of the Spirit and godly virtues that will enable you to be and achieve whatever your heart and hands set out to achieve.

Do you believe this can happen? Do you want it? If the answer to both is yes, let's get to work.

Mechanics of the Challenge

I decided to add details about the mechanics of the challenge (my thought process for coming up with it) because I hope it will help your commitment to participate and fully immerse yourself into it.

The number five carries great significance because it represents the grace of God. Know and believe there is a space of grace for you as you go through this 5-week challenge with the intention and conviction to complete it from start to finish.

But what I know for sure is you must *want* to participate. You must *want* to fully engage. You must *want* to care and concern yourself about improving your use of words, your self talk. And in order to get to this level of want and subsequent aligning behavior, it must be in your heart. When you get your heart set on something, then it's game on.

But even still, when your heart is in it, this challenge will not be a cake walk. Controlling what we say and how we say it (especially in heated, highly emotional states) is one of the most difficult things to do within our being. The author of the book of James in the bible describes the tongue as a world of unrighteousness.

However with intention and becoming more spiritual in your thinking and actions, we can speak good that begets abundant life and abundant living.

But back to the mechanics of the challenge. The challenge is, for 5 weeks, to show up every day at the same time to speak aloud the daily self talk for that day. Showing up at the same time is key.

While this may seem simple, it requires conviction, commitment and an ample amount of self-discipline. So much that my first and second attempts at this were fails. I would show up strong and consistent for a few days up until a little over a week then become inconsistent until I fell off completely. When I didn't show up, either I was too busy or I forgot to show up altogether. Can you say distracted and lack of focus? Ugh.

In hindsight, "too busy" was the excuse I used to let myself off the hook and when I forgot my bet is it was due to some fruitless distraction that was not more important than mastering my self talk and learning how to use words properly for what they are intended for.

Going back to the bible, life's best book of wisdom and instruction and the basis for science and every other discipline known to man, teaches us that our tongue is the smallest organ of our body yet the biggest to get control of. In fact, most human beings never do.

This book and challenge exist to change this.

Define Your Desired Outcomes of the Challenge

This challenge has been carefully thought out and designed to render the following outcomes and *more*. More in that the outcomes produced in you will be specific to where you are now starting off and where you want to be when you finish.

Use the extra space to add your desired outcomes now or later after you've started and things start to become clearer.

- To become more spiritual by the words you speak.
- To awaken your consciousness to the importance and power of the words you speak.
- To transform your heart; to truly care about the words you speak and the words you don't speak.
- To assign purpose to your words in order to produce what you desire to see in your being and, in turn, your life.
- To transform your responses from ill to elegant.
- To develop calmness, self-control and self-discipline.
- To develop habit, routine and consistency – the mother of all success.
- _____
- _____
- _____
- _____
- _____
- _____

The Pre-work: Self Coaching Questions

Before we dive in next, I want you to take some time to coach yourself in order to find out how open and receptive you are to spiritual transformation through your words.

- Does the thought of becoming more spiritual move and/or inspire you?
- Do you remember the main reasons why becoming more spiritual is so vital to your 3B Self™?
- Do you believe becoming more spiritual is possible *just* by the words you speak?
- Do you believe this can be a reality *for you*?

If you answered yes to these questions keep reading and get ready for everything to begin to shift for you. Get ready for spiritual transformation into your highest and best self.

Challenge Instructions

While, as the author, I have some degree of influence over your thought process and subsequent actions you take from what I share, I fully trust and expect Holy Spirit to lead and steer you in this process. He knows exactly where you are and knows exactly what you need. Lean in and listen to Him first and foremost.

If you do not have a relationship with the Person of Holy Spirit, first, I encourage you to seek this out as doing so will change everything for you (both in this present age and hereafter) in ways you have never even thought or imagined.

Second to being led by a higher power, here are step-by-step instructions that can be followed in order to complete the challenge:

1. Pick your self-talk time.
    a. Decide when you will show up.
    b. Decide how long you will show up.
       (Note: 10 minutes is more than enough time but do what works for you)

2. Solidify your commitment by writing it down.
    a. After deciding when and how you will show up, write a note to yourself wherever you log the things you have to get done.

3. Act on your commitment.
    a. Schedule a recurring reminder or calendar event for your self-talk time

4. Self talk in isolation.
    a. Step away from all noise and distractions.
    b. Before you begin, take a minute to get centered by taking a few deep breaths. Shoot up a quick arrow prayer or whatever works to quiet your mind and calm your spirit. The goal is to be fully present and fully engaged mentally and physically, distraction free.

5. Start your self talk.
    a. When you speak, speak with conviction. Speak with zeal. Speak with power. Speak with authority. Speak from all these powerful attributes that stem from your strong and passionate belief in what you are speaking and the supernatural results they will render.

Challenge Format and Flow

The challenge is for 5 weeks, which is equal to 35 days. Each day includes the following four sections that are self-explanatory: Self Talk, Inspiration, Action and Reflection.

Further, I have added categories that can be thought of as "the big idea" for a given week. These categories are meant to help you understand the deeper significance and intention in your self talk as you go through each day of the challenge. Commit now to not skip ahead and rather consistently show up every day, preferably at the same time. Consider setting up a daily reminder in your phone.

Week	The Big Idea	The Deeper Intention
1	Being	Using your words to transform (awaken) your spirit.
2	Mindset	Using your words to transform (renew) your mindset.
3	Condition	Using your words to transform (Improve) your body.
4	Power	Using your words to transform (increase) your self-control when someone or something pushes your buttons.
5	Practice	Using your words to transform (establish) your consistency when it comes to your self-discipline aka daily routine.

Lastly, you should read each day out loud with belief and conviction, believing that what you are saying is true for you now because the words you are speaking are transforming you. Real-time transformation. Real-time transformation. Real-time transformation.

Are you ready for it? If so, let's go!

BEING

Day 1: The Best Part of Me

SELF TALK
I acknowledge and exalt my spirit, which is the best part of me made in the image and likeness of my Creator, God the Father.

INSPIRATION
Genesis 1:27

ACTION
1. Reflect. Write out any mental feedback to this self talk
2. Repeat. Speak this self talk for the remainder of the day

REFLECTION

_____

_____

_____

BEING

Day 2: The Place Where I Belong

SELF TALK

I abide in the present moment which is absent of fears, worries, hurts, bad habits and hang-ups. I am free in the present moment.

INSPIRATION

Matthew 6:25-34

ACTION

1. Reflect. Write out any mental feedback to this self talk
2. Repeat. Speak this self talk for the remainder of the day

REFLECTION

_____

_____

_____

BEING

Day 3: Peace is My Inheritance

SELF TALK
I receive the inner peace that has been given to me. I decree total peace within myself and for everything that concerns me.

INSPIRATION
John 14:27

ACTION
1. Reflect. Write out any mental feedback to this self talk
2. Repeat. Speak this self talk for the remainder of the day

REFLECTION

_____

_____

_____

BEING

Day 4: Staying in My Lane

SELF TALK

To strive is to step outside my lane. Rather, the related characteristic of my spirit is calm and as a spirit being I flow naturally.

INSPIRATION

Psalm 46:10

ACTION

1. Reflect. Write out any mental feedback to this self talk
2. Repeat. Speak this self talk for the remainder of the day

REFLECTION

_____

_____

_____

_____

BEING

Day 5: Soul Currency

SELF TALK

My inner being breeds contentment, the currency of my soul. Regardless of any past and/or present experience, the superior truth is I am perfectly perfect and completely complete. My well-being always has been and always will be an inside job.

INSPIRATION
1 Timothy 6:6

ACTION
1. Reflect. Write out any mental feedback to this self talk
2. Repeat. Speak this self talk for the remainder of the day

REFLECTION

_____

_____

_____

_____

BEING

Day 6: Beyond Choosing Joy

SELF TALK

Contrary to popular expression, joy is not just something I choose. Like peace, joy is an inheritance of mine. As such, I am full of it. I am the embodiment of joy unspeakable.

INSPIRATION
John 15:11

ACTION
1. Reflect. Write out any mental feedback to this self talk
2. Repeat. Speak this self talk for the remainder of the day

REFLECTION

_____

_____

_____

_____

BEING

Day 7: The Word as Bread

SELF TALK

My unseen inner man requires spiritual meat. I do not fail to feed my spirit. The Word of God is my bread. I feed on it daily.

INSPIRATION
Matthew 4:4

ACTION
1. Reflect. Write out any mental feedback to this self talk
2. Repeat. Speak this self talk for the remainder of the day

REFLECTION

_____

_____

_____

_____

MINDSET

Day 8: Habitual Mental Checkup's

SELF TALK
With conviction and intention, I check every perspective that comes to my mind against the light of truth as revealed in the Bible.

INSPIRATION
Matthew 4:17

ACTION
1. Reflect. Write out any mental feedback to this self talk
2. Repeat. Speak this self talk for the remainder of the day

REFLECTION

_____

_____

_____

MINDSET

Day 9: Forget the Status Quo

SELF TALK

I no longer align my reasoning with tradition, popular opinion or how family, close friends or colleagues think. My thoughts agree with the heartbeats of Heaven – Father, Son and Holy Spirit.

INSPIRATION

Romans 12:2

ACTION

1. Reflect. Write out any mental feedback to this self talk
2. Repeat. Speak this self talk for the remainder of the day

REFLECTION

_____

_____

_____

_____

MINDSET

Day 10: Modus Operandi X

SELF TALK

I acknowledge the faculty and function of my thoughts, whether operating based on truth or deception, is what will determine my actions and outcomes today – whether they will be good or evil.

INSPIRATION
John 8:42-47

ACTION
1. Reflect. Write out any mental feedback to this self talk
2. Repeat. Speak this self talk for the remainder of the day

REFLECTION

_____

_____

_____

_____

MINDSET

Day 11: In the New

SELF TALK

I am a new person with a new nature because my thoughts are new and are continually being renewed.

INSPIRATION

Ephesians 4:23

ACTION

1. Reflect. Write out any mental feedback to this self talk
2. Repeat. Speak this self talk for the remainder of the day

REFLECTION

_____

_____

_____

_____

MINDSET

Day 12: Being Spiritually Minded

SELF TALK

Today and every day in my thoughts (and words and actions that follow), I choose life and peace over death and chaos.

INSPIRATION
Romans 8:6

ACTION
1. Reflect. Write out any mental feedback to this self talk
2. Repeat. Speak this self talk for the remainder of the day

REFLECTION

_____
_____
_____
_____

MINDSET

Day 13: The Way Up is Down

SELF TALK

I choose to think (and thus walk) in the way of humility understanding self-exaltation is the highest form of deception and truly the way up is actually down.

INSPIRATION

Philippians 2:5

ACTION

1. Reflect. Write out any mental feedback to this self talk
2. Repeat. Speak this self talk for the remainder of the day

REFLECTION

_____

_____

_____

_____

MINDSET

Day 14: Where Freedom Is

SELF TALK
I fill my mind with truth because I understand every physical bondage is rooted in mental deception and the entrance of truth brings freedom.

INSPIRATION
John 8:31-32

ACTION
1. Reflect. Write out any mental feedback to this self talk
2. Repeat. Speak this self talk for the remainder of the day

REFLECTION

_____

_____

_____

_____

CONDITION

Day 15: Matters of the Heart

SELF TALK

I realize my spiritual and physical condition are both the result and outflow of the condition of my heart. I examine my heart daily in light of God's Word.

INSPIRATION
Proverbs 4:23

ACTION
1. Reflect. Write out any mental feedback to this self talk
2. Repeat. Speak this self talk for the remainder of the day

REFLECTION

_____

_____

_____

CONDITION

Day 16: Receiving Glory

SELF TALK

With boldness and confidence, I receive the glory that belongs to me in Christ from Christ and from the Father.

INSPIRATION

John 17:22

ACTION

1. Reflect. Write out any mental feedback to this self talk
2. Repeat. Speak this self talk for the remainder of the day

REFLECTION

_____

_____

_____

_____

CONDITION

Day 17: Increasing Glory

SELF TALK

I lower and humble myself as, through the work of the Spirit in me, corruption decreases and God's glory increases.

INSPIRATION
2 Corinthians 3:18

ACTION
1. Reflect. Write out any mental feedback to this self talk
2. Repeat. Speak this self talk for the remainder of the day

REFLECTION

_____
_____
_____
_____

CONDITION

Day 18: Crowned with Glory

SELF TALK

As it is written about me, I am crowned with glory and honor and I commit to speaking and acting in alignment with this godly virtue.

INSPIRATION
Psalms 8:5

ACTION
1. Reflect. Write out any mental feedback to this self talk
2. Repeat. Speak this self talk for the remainder of the day

REFLECTION

_____

_____

_____

_____

CONDITION

Day 19: Called to Glory

SELF TALK

Today and every day I commit to use my words and subsequent actions in ways that are worthy of the call of God to His glory.

INSPIRATION

1 Thessalonians 2:12

ACTION

1. Reflect. Write out any mental feedback to this self talk
2. Repeat. Speak this self talk for the remainder of the day

REFLECTION

_____

_____

_____

_____

CONDITION

Day 20: The Image of Glory

SELF TALK

As it is written of me, I accept and boldly proclaim I am the image and the glory of God.

INSPIRATION

1 Corinthians 11:7

ACTION

1. Reflect. Write out any mental feedback to this self talk
2. Repeat. Speak this self talk for the remainder of the day

REFLECTION

_____

_____

_____

_____

CONDITION

Day 21: Flesh and Bones

SELF TALK

One of the major ways in which I keep my body healthy is by having and holding words of Wisdom and Truth in my heart.

INSPIRATION
Proverbs 4:20-22

ACTION
1. Reflect. Write out any mental feedback to this self talk
2. Repeat. Speak this self talk for the remainder of the day

REFLECTION

_____

_____

_____

_____

POWER

Day 22: My Superior Self

SELF TALK

Today and every day I embrace the superiority of my spirit because I recognize the more spiritual I become the more powerful I become.

INSPIRATION

Galatians 5:16

ACTION

1. Reflect. Write out any mental feedback to this self talk
2. Repeat. Speak this self talk for the remainder of the day

REFLECTION

_____

_____

_____

_____

POWER

Day 23: The Spirit of Life

SELF TALK

Abiding in the Spirit of Life nourishes the best part of me (my spirit) and from this place I am empowered to live in total freedom and victory.

INSPIRATION

Romans 8:2

ACTION

1. Reflect. Write out any mental feedback to this self talk
2. Repeat. Speak this self talk for the remainder of the day

REFLECTION

_____

_____

_____

_____

POWER

Day 24: Receiving Holy Spirit

SELF TALK

I acknowledge and receive the Person of the Holy Spirit who fills me with dynamite-like power and might so I can do good works and overcome evil works.

INSPIRATION
Acts 1:8

ACTION
1. Reflect. Write out any mental feedback to this self talk
2. Repeat. Speak this self talk for the remainder of the day

REFLECTION

_____

_____

_____

_____

POWER

Day 25: Experiencing Holy Spirit

SELF TALK

I invite the Person of Holy Spirit to fully work in me by continually emptying myself of pride, ego and all other ugly self-centered traits.

INSPIRATION

John 3:30 and Ephesians 3:20

ACTION

1. Reflect. Write out any mental feedback to this self talk
2. Repeat. Speak this self talk for the remainder of the day

REFLECTION

_____

_____

_____

_____

POWER

Day 26: Bodily Sacrifice

SELF TALK

I present my body as a living sacrifice because nothing good dwells in my flesh. I live from my spirit, the best part of me like God.

INSPIRATION

Romans 7:18,12:2 and Colossians 3:5,10

ACTION

1. Reflect. Write out any mental feedback to this self talk
2. Repeat. Speak this self talk for the remainder of the day

REFLECTION

_____

_____

_____

_____

POWER

Day 27: Produce and Performance

SELF TALK

For my assignment today, I understand the way in which I will produce the most and perform the best is by abiding in the Spirit.

INSPIRATION
John 15:5

ACTION
1. Reflect. Write out any mental feedback to this self talk
2. Repeat. Speak this self talk for the remainder of the day

REFLECTION

_____
_____
_____
_____

POWER

Day 28: A Necessary Exchange

SELF TALK

I acknowledge and exchange my human weaknesses by wholly turning to the Spirit for the strength He delights to provide for me.

INSPIRATION

Romans 8:26

ACTION

1. Reflect. Write out any mental feedback to this self talk
2. Repeat. Speak this self talk for the remainder of the day

REFLECTION

_____

_____

_____

PRACTICE

Day 29: Training My Body

SELF TALK

I understand while exercising self-discipline feels painful, the gain is always much greater than any pain involved. So I keep pressing in.

INSPIRATION

Hebrews 12:11

ACTION

1. Reflect. Write out any mental feedback to this self talk
2. Repeat. Speak this self talk for the remainder of the day

REFLECTION

_____

_____

_____

_____

PRACTICE

Day 30: Conditioning My Soul

SELF TALK

Every day I choose to endure the difficulty of self-discipline and/or sacrifice of some sort knowing my ultimate reward will be eternally golden and glorious.

INSPIRATION

1 Corinthians 9:27

ACTION

1. Reflect. Write out any mental feedback to this self talk
2. Repeat. Speak this self talk for the remainder of the day

REFLECTION

_____

_____

_____

_____

PRACTICE

Day 31: Singing Words in My Heart

SELF TALK
Today I will sing a lyrically beautiful and joyful song held in my heart as a part of my regular speak and vocabulary of words.

INSPIRATION
Ephesians 5:19-20

ACTION
1. Reflect. Write out any mental feedback to this self talk
2. Repeat. Speak this self talk for the remainder of the day

REFLECTION

_____
_____
_____
_____

PRACTICE

Day 32: Speaking Words of Truth

SELF TALK
Today I verbally ask for the desires of my heart that align with the desires and heart of my heavenly Father. Desires based on Truth.

INSPIRATION
John 15:7

ACTION
1. Reflect. Write out any mental feedback to this self talk
2. Repeat. Speak this self talk for the remainder of the day

REFLECTION

_____

_____

_____

_____

PRACTICE

Day 33: Keeping Watch Over My Words

SELF TALK
I am careful about what I say and how I say it. I choose my words wisely because they greatly impact my health and well-being.

INSPIRATION
Proverbs 21:23

ACTION
1. Reflect. Write out any mental feedback to this self talk
2. Repeat. Speak this self talk for the remainder of the day

REFLECTION

_____

_____

_____

PRACTICE

Day 34: Activating My Spirit

SELF TALK

I am intentional and uncompromising about thanksgiving and engaging my being in activities that are joyful, uplifting and edifying.

INSPIRATION

1 Thessalonians 5:16-18

ACTION

1. Reflect. Write out any mental feedback to this self talk
2. Repeat. Speak this self talk for the remainder of the day

REFLECTION

_____
_____
_____
_____

PRACTICE

Day 35: Praying Without Ceasing

SELF TALK

I acknowledge and embrace prayer as a vital part of my spirit being and I devote myself to a moment-by-moment posture of prayer.

INSPIRATION
Colossians 4:2

ACTION
1. Reflect. Write out any mental feedback to this self talk
2. Repeat. Speak this self talk for the remainder of the day

REFLECTION

_____

_____

_____

_____

Part 4: Conclusion

Hopefully you are reading these words having just finished Day 35 of the 5-week Self Talk challenge that was thoughtfully designed to make you more spiritual by the words you speak. If so, this cute little something extra I decided to include is especially for you:

You did it! I do not say this lightly, that you should be extremely proud of yourself for showing up and completing each day of this challenge – even if you missed a day or days for whatever reason and had to catch up. Remember I failed twice.

So, for all who finish, what I know for sure is you are a rare human being with a high calling. Even after getting the revelations shared in parts 1 and 2 of the book, most will still not develop the conviction that creates the needed consistency to finish something of this nature.

Why? Because it is absent of sensual raw feel gratification that most of humanity craves and, tragically, give chase to. And no this is not me being negative or pessimistic or condescending or judgmental or self-righteous or anything of the sort. Far from it. This is me calling out, in love, the reality of what is with hope and action for change.

One hundred percent, love is the underlying motivation for me sharing my voice about words and how to become better in our 3B Self™ (being/body/behavior) by using them aright.

The Way Forward

Knowing what we now know about words. Now that our consciousness has been awakened or raised. Now that a deep passion has hopefully formed in our hearts that causes us to truly be concerned and to truly care about how we use our words and to not be so willy-nilly with them. Now that we understand the creative power of our words. Now that we understand the consequences that come from how we choose to use our words. What is the way forward? How ought we to speak henceforth?

As an important reminder and important ending thought, the intention and purpose of the challenge was so you could develop a spiritual practice. Really think about this idea of spiritual practice.

In this day in age where information and technology and artificial intelligence and everything in society turning digital, we human beings (keyword *beings*, not machines) need to have spiritual practices that keep will keep us grounded in our humanity and thereby maintaining our godliness – which is our makeup in the image and likeness of our Creator God the Father.

Too, spiritual practices work to transform us into something greater. If you are an artist or athlete or are a fan of an artist or athlete of any kind, you understand practice plays an essential role in the making of that great artist or athlete. Without practice and the inherent, inseparable discipline that comes along with it, you or whoever would not be a great artist or athlete.

Practice, self-discipline, self-sacrifice, and consistency all go together and are honored and rewarded by men and, moreover, honored and rewarded by God Himself.

Now being further awake to this and everything that has been shared, as you go forward in your being and life, keep top of mind how self talk is an avenue for you and your children and your children's children and so on to be and become your and their highest and best selves. Because, recall, we are the only creatures (man) throughout all creation given the privilege to use words like God.

With this great privilege comes great responsibility:

- The responsibility to care deeply about how we use words.
- The responsibility to do the self work within ourselves so we are empowered to use self-restraint with our words whenever needed.
- The responsibility to pattern our words after our Creator and use them how He does and how He instructs us to use them.
- The responsibility to use our words to create our world for the glory and honor of God.

Finally, speaking of privilege and responsibility, it has been mine to have walked with you on this journey. Let's commit to staying on the right course with our words and reach success together. Cheers!

Terri Andres

About The Author

Terri Andres is a woman of great passion, purpose and influence who has given her whole self and life to service. At the age of 23, she was radically saved and transformed into a brand new person through a supernatural encounter with God. Today, Terri is a formally trained minister in the Christian faith, a gifted communicator, visionary, entrepreneur, and cheerful giver. When she is not working, she is enjoying life with her husband Hal and their adult children and families.

Visit harvester-publishing.com to get the other two books in this powerful *Self Series* volume.

Self Series Book I

Self-Control: Power to Experience Breakthrough, Transformation and New Life

Living with self-control means living with *POWER!*

- Power to resist anything that is resisting you
- Power to overcome any obstacle
- Power to experience breakthroughs to new levels and heights you have only dreamed of
- Power to take action and not just any action but the right action
- Power to persevere and remain consistent
- Power to create anything you can think of
- Power to reach your maximum potential
- And, last but certainly not least, power to fulfill your God-given purpose in the earth

This book is 300 pages of knowledge and practical application that is guaranteed to change your life!

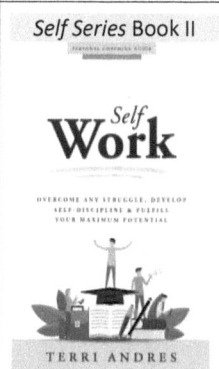

Self Series Book II

Self Work: Overcome Any Struggle, Develop Self-Discipline & Fulfill Your Maximum Potential

- Better health & well-being start with a better self
- Better relationships start with a better self
- Better finances start with a better self
- Better business and career start with a better self

When you do the self work first, everything else will work. It is time to flip the script and focus on *you* instead of what you do. This 200-page personal coaching guide will lead you to the "better" you need!

www.ingramcontent.com/pod-product-compliance
Lightning Source LLC
Chambersburg PA
CBHW060402080526
44583CB00012B/441